THE ORCHARD GREEN AND EVERY COLOR

Zach Savich

THE ORCHARD GREEN AND EVERY COLOR

OMNIDAWN PUBLISHING
OAKLAND, CALIFORNIA
2016

Cover art by Christina P. Day: Outlook #1, Found object, photographic decal, 1.75" x 1.75" x .5", 2007; courtesy of the artist. www.chrissyday.com.

Typefaces: Century Gothic, Garamond, and Gill Sans Std

Cover and Interior Design by Sharon Zetter

Offset printed in the United States
by Edwards Brothers Malloy, Ann Arbor, Michigan
On 55# Heritage Book Cream White Antique

Library of Congress Cataloging-in-Publication Data
Names: Savich, Zach.
Title: The orchard green and every color / Zach Savich.
Description: Oakland, California : Omnidawn Publishing, 2016.
Identifiers: LCCN 2015040580 | ISBN 9781632430182 (pbk. : alk. paper)
Classification: LCC PS3619.A858 A6 2016 | DDC 811/.6--dc23
LC record available at http://lccn.loc.gov/2015040580

Published by Omnidawn Publishing, Oakland, California
www.omnidawn.com   (510) 237-5472   (800) 792-4957
10 9 8 7 6 5 4 3 2 1
ISBN: 978-1-63243-013-7

Contents

for Hilary

My Summer Hospital

Or days bounty exaggerated the labor's strain

Grapes thread on a thigh

Has not thirst made the nectar run

And savory the acorn

My elegy is just ongoing consciousness

Trail maintained by flood

I wake early enough to see those whose work begins before heat

Heat precedes me

Wind where the chimes will be

Beautiful, in a passing way

Thus, more beautiful the more it passes me

Much as those birds that never touch the ground

Is this tree the ground

Is fruit the ground

There's little evidence of the bee's contact with the blossom

Outside the blossom

By alternating crops, you make toil easy

Cardinal in some stacked panes, or in each of them

In my time travel dream, we agree to visit the present

My pose is known as The Hopelessly Open Gate

Be quiet, no one wants to hear you, says the man on his porch to his pug

It's what he always says

I always say hello

He knows the year

Days I effortlessly memorized

You don't need to paint faces in the trees

There are faces already

Today is an open letter

Read it to me

To everything, lemon added

This appetite doesn't signal deficiency

The final step of transplanting is distress the trunk

One with a hose kept the dust heavy, in demolition

Flower in a plastic water bottle

Which came first

Radio on the neighbor's porch giving the weather

Is the weather

Walked to the supermart

Three women in the parking lot, praying for someone in the hospital

Who *Lord you'd be wrong to think is just anybody*

A Different Year

FIRST POSITION

I have been practicing a knot so complex the rope goes completely straight at times

SNOW SALE

The only seasonal fruit,

Perfect berries

We've been picked early and sliced thin

Near vines one hoped to trick

Into subsequent flourishing

In this place where families from town

Shovel snow into pick-ups, and descend

From this place where every step

Is elevation

I sit on my bench

and disperse with the train crowd

you know these are cherries by the rough bark

also the fruit

you know a tree fell here

by how finely saplings grew

now take a consequential breath

the wedge you cut has all the lemon's juice

nest held by feathers moving in it

my eyes have no color but what they saw

BENCHES IN A SMALL BACKYARD

Which tradition is waking

Most traditions

Which planet is the sun

I walk beneath the music

Salt marsh

Platelets

Braided grain ends, as though there is order

Beneath the hangdog tree and pronged goose honk

I have lived among leaves in equal part turned, turning, and green

the landscape isn't over

they put seeds in the walls

of the disintegrating home

it has made a field worth looking for

planks held by shaped wire

spent mill

brickwork undeniably skilled

even in struts and frames no one could have seen

it is February

or July

all you can predict about a year from now

the date

ALSO AND ALWAYS

I write you from a peripheral grown large enough

To rest in or turn around

Tell me with a look

The tires will go flat and there is a restaurant called Open

Much as one practicing an instrument

Inadvertently comes into song and stays there

But also: here is a late love poem, in the style of this fire escape they painted through the best they could, so yellow slashes the siding. Chestnuts you can break by hand, against other chestnuts in your hand.

On the hazed lawn one tosses leaves saved or found unbrowned beneath some fallen thing. A minor, mythic re-enactment of fall I'd nevertheless call beautiful, as the sadly elaborate texturing of a hall can make plain notes, briefly, orchestral.

And another thing: the first globes were clay orbs. Sailors affixed new continents by thumbing a percent of a sphere's core out and pressing a lobe of land, or pinched mountain, or antelope.

Now past this field where they rest anything until there's enough and auction it.

Ladders lean out second-level windows. Day passing out. Leaflets.

The smallest strip beside the house: a garden.

I LAPSE

A man on whom some snows no longer fall

I could polish the boards until they blossom again

Cut stems suspended in a vase,
The eyes

Cut stems suspended
In a blue and quartz-planed vase

HOWEVER EARLY WE WAKE IS MORNING

Hour before vendors are allowed to sell

Join in soccer at the market's edge

Is this tree the goal

Should we continue chasing down the street

Let it be morning whenever you read

A person calling into the pines

Here,

A name,

And *here*

Small stalks

In an emptied barrow

the eye still winds at any climbing thing

calls it *ivy*

it's ivy then

each season made to see

I wake clean and used

lattice braced in the amaryllis bed

each motion shaped

did the waist begin in the throat

if the hands

if the hands began in the breath

so one heaved one

restrained

a scent of rain perhaps

perhaps for days

in the makeshift delphiniums

on the makeshift weight bench

a yard conveying primed assent

if the hair began

if the eyes

so the place that felt the most

made all the others feel

A HOUSE CALLED FIRE

The sense I've wanted only lasts a day

Ivy on an alley wall

To teach somebody to build a fire
You can give them an axe or make them cold

They might build a house

If you have already labeled the photograph
The house will be called *Fire*

Ivy on an alley wall

I can't be alone in this

more and more I appreciate the stone tower's bell

which strikes once for half-past

and doesn't bother with the hours

notes do not stop

yet so much happens between

I bring my friend two apples and a stone

I rest in shade from leaves the window lets in

under clouds the color of clouds birds have been in

darker in the morning and at dusk

stranger to the touch

anything seen

being outside the body

is plainly ecstasy

DAY NAMED FIRMAMENT

New rust: a fertile and promising orange

Was the first word *instead*

Was the first word *especially now*

The purpose still being able to say

Purpose or *being*

My steamship needs nothing but the steam it makes

Moving over the water

Clover can take it from here

Windows boarded with the prettiest wood. And the separated maple syrup colors of a forever for sale truck.

As one carrying a heavy load walks quicker so momentum balances, not to speed his end, I watched them tear shingles from the roof, keeping their footing any way they could, and their momentum balanced me. They crouched above me, some high red berries still on the trees, dusk darkening them faster at that height, as though darkening up from the house they opened.

In place of a radio, one man sang a little—*I held your hand so I would never end*—with a voice that, untrained, trained his listeners. When they climbed down he was the one they shook the ladder for.

TO LOVE IMPLIES TOO MUCH

Open the window

I want to mistake freshness for warmth

The physical day awash with larkspur

Everything I remember happened at once

Gold flying in, in summer

So what—it is summer and the leaves are falling

In one version, she grew her hair lushly through the noose

So she could sing a little longer

And the acrobat cut his net into a hundred capes

And all our instruments are green

HEAVEN FOR A DOLLAR

But this is a longer story, about a tree that grew

When the window near it opened

And someone you saw leaned out

Also, there is a hardness at the center of the bale

While small flowers ache the exterior

Also, tomatoes so small they've already burst

By when they're visible

tied in the second inning

the young catcher calms his pitcher

crocuses enameling the outfield

ersatz mockingbird

I cover my eyes wanting every car yours

where the road stalls out in unwreathed posts

and flowers to the edge

PERHAPS BIRDS

I don't trust my tears

I trust first

They follow

Hay bits blown to camber vetch in sporadic steam

There is no window I can open without touching leaves

Staved, and near to heave

Beside the delicate auburn fretwork

Of perhaps birds

Easy as a gate latched by a length of weathered yarn

once more aloft

or is it once more heaves

dark fuses fueled through

loosening a hinge one borrowed cup

of flour's width

I pinch the wick

and glimpse: white grasses

palindrome of ocher brush

thundercloud with the threadcount

of a squash blossom

I picture you in a house it arouses you to rent

(there are people

aroused by a home)

neighbor rakes his stoop

some kids have spray-painted a fetus

onto a mailbox

small slanders of snow

geese jolt from the open backs of billboards

if you can ask in a glance

the mind a zagging bramble of iron filings

seized tender behind the brow

EXIT CENTRIFUGE

I'm hotter than a raspberry in a wineglass

You can go off the road wherever you like

These real colors: lovely and rapt and small evergreen

What warmth is unseasonable

I lift from lower than the knees
I wipe my sweat with a hotter cloth

I look for the source of the echo
I see an arrangement of sky

Videos onto windows. Marquees. I have been hired to pretend to
photograph.

Casual immolation of the hesitant exchange…

Preliminaries on the patio, the genial squander of a public afternoon…

Flowers packed in telegrams and ice. Please remove the flowers.

The most again, or once more again, and more than ever. And what now won't come to seem like innocence, and extradition. Pleasure educates.

A single strand of onion in the dough gave savor.

Longevity in the violin student's bow, fixed in its case. She thumbed a string.

Painted the boarded windows white, so snow.

SCRAP GOLD

Then all was vineyard, all was grape

Kept a bone in the oven so the heat learned depth

The implosions have been slow and restful ever since

Clothesline is a sentence

Or snowbank

We spoke, as birds unsettled in the trees outside

We spoke, much as birds that unsettle

Yet do not lift, yet seem to move the trees

They built the cathedral with a battered door

Canoe forever on a car

CACTUS ON A METAL STAIR

Low bees alert in the first cold

The leaves that turn first last longest

Near a barbed wire fence
With the fence part gone

You can just walk under

Dry vines on the wire

A question is saying yes

Or to measure the distance
By a mossed tennis
Ball on the path

Lavender grown back long before that

one evening discerns

earthiness and abruptly reasonless elation

time and again and time

and another time

the quarried brown marquee

of today's maples

deceives sufficiently

say the trapeze artist removes his harness

shutters off their hinges lean

against a foregone view

and the lichen of the endocrine

breaks into its corralled trot

in breaking rain

if we get gas here we can hear

the station you like a little longer

WHICH SIDE OF THE LAKE IS LONGEST

We put the musicians in the prettiest room

Usually is enough

Instruments stirring at the touch of any air

As air provides a bottle's final taste
(*Let the vintage breathe…*)

I could raise the clothesline for the long gowns

My neighborhood is closer on foot

I trust most the later promises

in which we do not promise what we will do

and we do not promise

what we will never do again

we promise what we are

affectionately building up

additions to an unzoned home

to reach the newest room

step through any wall

TUESDAY

Delighted to hear the child say

What is my first name

What is my second name

And her mother spelled it

Zarina Richardson

Beside me on the train

I resolved to stand where the light was

Green where the light was

In the evening in the trees

Like another decade's imagining

Of another century

The hammering down the street does not have a cause

My hands' lines have grown undefined: grasses in their wires, fancy fishing knots, bones of a stray. The hard to handle can be sweet to see?

I whisper the harder notes. The snow was dirty until it fell.

School buses learning their routes, late August. Tiger lilies animate in a ditch. If you fail as a waiter, the restaurant may hire you as a singer.

ENOUGH AS YOU LIKE

The clarity of the last steeping

I've made this bitter to assure the pleasure

Of adding cream

My creamy bitterness

Evening more a stance than an hour

Different laundry cold on the line

Because of where I grew

Water is always west

THE BUNDLED ROOTS OF SAPLINGS

I write you from the afterlife

Hills mint-moistened, breezing about

As recipes on a fridge in earliest summer

There is an orchard under this

Flower ships

Saplings with their bundled roots

Starting already to bear

heaviest the hand that holds the plow still

plantation pines filament the shore

I wished for the excesses of my age
and I wished for more eternal excesses
and wanted to be implicated more
and warmed my hands
indefinitely
in fists

and my body felt like something else again
heart hardened to move swifter in the sluice
by a hedge held straight by bent branches
my body also is

fire hydrant trickling down
through construction dust
nickel-soft and trussed
through constant strain
and elegant intensity
it patterns an expanse
will put nothing out

TWO WEEKS AND ONE DAY

The pose known as celestial (eyes skyward)

Anchors (you have to love the earth a lot

To have to look away)

Much as the right appetite

Turns excess into abundance,

Difficulty into a kind of ease

Because total

Where I have been run through

There is no wound, only open air

The taste on my tongue is not too sweet

It's simply sugar

Also, the day looks lovely on you

It looks like what, in landscape,

They call the advantage, where one habitat

Blushes into another

And birds there can storm the meadow

Or sing

Also, nothing is free and lasts forever

Seeing you is like seeing somebody I already adore

In a perfect shirt

dry marsh overdone with clovers

lake the color of a good claret

aged a day too long

a good chef adjusts the soup around

heaviest the hand that stills the plow

the drowned man's shirt

did not dry

until all had given their respects

FOR ALL WE KNOW

Behind my eyes are the long stones that keep a field unplanted

So the fertile top is pristine

I say *pleasure*

I say *escalate*

Knowing little but faithful to the little green even dew sets off

I stay one step ahead of my gaze

It's all right, I'm in there, and it's all reunion

Any moment now is some other time

Good night. I know. I know. I know.

The hospital door is wide enough for a carried bed, and a wing is half a shore.

It was late in the instants of a children's game. If you step in any shadow, even your own, you must follow it to the end.

My father entertained the smarter ones by multiplying darkness on the lawn.

He said, *There is a shadow under every length of grass, even in your eyes, in the center of* (flourish) *this match, in reeds grown close, then pulled away, but not before ice fixed them to the paint, even in your eyes*—until the game, meshed in suggestion, turned to simple seeing.

BOATS COLLECT AT THE MOUTH

I curl a vine as though that cares for the vine

Too small to be displaced

Place pulling weeds

Pries free the bricks

Stars out
Tall as a clawfoot tub

Has my orgy been too apparent
Is my painting snow

The things I like are the things that happen

Cut once,
Measure

THE WORLD WILL NOT BE MADE AGAIN IN ANY OF ITS EARLIER WAYS

Spared, yet proud to have been

Near enough, a time,

To have wished to be spared

The distance between us has been consistent,

But I have thinned, so it's worth more to me

Sweetness remains the source of sweetness

But now I prefer the vase's resonant hollow

To any exterior fractures

Will you be long

Is years long

Is long enough any time at all

I've traded my instruments for a song

quite literally

the etymology of fathom is

extend your arms

each august they unsettle

a basket of petals in the nave

it honors the unseasonable snow

that named the church

and what city has the honor of providing the petals

and who has the honor of overturning them

outside the magician is still assembling his crowd

he has them cheer

drawing others in

they applaud the barest moon

ENVELOPE

One paints precisely the worn

If given an entire life,

Perhaps…

But if given a day, or any day…

I hold the gate a moment before settling the latch

Early advice: don't say *silence*,

Say *distance* twice

They wanted an encore so they could throw their flowers

The leaves don't need to break the window

I can see them where they are

still-blown

the barrage

softens me down

a lifetime at this age

little to redeem

and less to shore

unsure which marrings of the façade

were the famed

ravages of war

and which were made

by an initial architect

for authenticity

a barbarian might note and serenely spare

QUIET AS BASEBALL OVER THE RADIO

Emulsification is a better model

Rome leads to all roads

Easy to see as impossible to see enough

But now I prefer the moment the back fence blocks

The florist conveying flowers, so there's this hovering

Floral procession

Most guidebooks are guidebooks to any city

Anything is a way to keep a flower living longer

The transliteration of *kestrel* is wind-fucker

I have been standing with a kite so large

Who can tell what's kite

What's wind

What's string

My sister colors the air between birds: the color of flight. This month she distinguishes between beaks and feathers, not by switching crayons, but by rubbing hard through the paper to make the beaks opening.

I parked far to walk.

The skin peels back with ripening. Now point to where exactly in the brain you believe this so-called light begins.

I stand under a tree I can identify if it flowers.

shed red at dusk

then white again in the redder sky

tomatoes where the tulips were

meadow in every

unmown angle

the neighbor boy whips

a rope against a barn wall

the paint has come away to look

like anyone's portrait as a patch of ill-formed light

anyone's portrait as a mess of boards

it's not the dying but the disentangling

and every death is young

trail demands crossing many creeks

demands pausing near the home with a chained drive

they are selling cauliflower

just before the chain

having lived enough

any coincidence is ordinary

I suppose somebody lived

on every street

as so often on meeting

the dead the dead ask *what are you*

and you could answer anything

but usually say *alive*

of all the metamorphoses I can never remember

what people turn into but why

snow in the cistern

so often the dead in apartments

in other parts of this city

spoken to fantastically or distantly all this time

so one dies and what has changed

much as cooking well becomes

not calculation or performance of arduous craft

but any evening now

rather than a conclusive month

hour the restaurant owners dine

bottle excessive enough to exchange for a meal

nothing lost

over the tracks

straining as though if you strain

you can see

any train

I don't mind it late

given such a tremendous sail

who alive would mind

who alive would mind

who alive would mind

the smallness of our boat

tremendously flayed

shirt cinched in a window

signaling

come to me here or

one is already with me here or

said *faith should be in the figuring*

out after

advised looking back coming in so you'll know

what it looks like coming back

and if you don't come back at least

you'll know how it could have seemed

one popular game is name the first thing you think

you'll never see again

then see more like it

bare nail a branch

ankles crossed to hold

the portioned berries

a different year

Acknowledgments

I am grateful to the editors of the following journals:

AMERICAN POETRY REVIEW

BERFROIS

BUFFALO NEWS

COLORADO REVIEW

FACT-SIMILE

FIRST RESPONSE

FOURTEEN HILLS

GHOST PROPOSAL

GREEN MOUNTAINS REVIEW

LAUREL REVIEW

NOO

PANGYRUS

PHILADELPHIA REVIEW OF BOOKS

POETRY NORTHWEST

PROPELLOR

PROTEUS

STRANGE MACHINE

TRANSOM

ZACH SAVICH is the author of the poetry collections *Full Catastrophe Living* (University of Iowa, 2009), *Annulments* (Center for Literary Publishing, 2010), *The Firestorm* (Cleveland State University Poetry Center, 2011), and *Century Swept Brutal* (Black Ocean, 2013). His work has appeared in journals and anthologies including *American Poetry Review*, *A Public Space*, and *Best New Poets*. He has received the Iowa Poetry Prize, the Colorado Prize for Poetry, Omnidawn's Chapbook Prize, and the Cleveland State University Poetry Center's Open Award, among other honors. Savich teaches in the BFA Program for Creative Writing at the University of the Arts, in Philadelphia, and co-edits Rescue Press's Open Prose Series.

The Orchard Green and Every Color
by Zach Savich

Cover art by Christina P. Day:
Outlook #1, Found object, photographic decal,
1.75" x 1.75" x .5", 2007; courtesy of the artist. www.chrissyday.com.

Cover text set in Century Gothic and Gill Sans Std
Interior text set in Century Gothic and Garamond Pro

Cover and Interior Design by Sharon Zetter

Offset printed in the United States
by Edwards Brothers Malloy, Ann Arbor, Michigan
On 55# Heritage Book Cream White Antique

Publication of this book was made possible in part by gifts from:
Robin & Curt Caton
John Gravendyk

Omnidawn Publishing
Richmond, California
2016

Rusty Morrison & Ken Keegan, senior editors & co-publishers
Gillian Olivia Blythe Hamel, managing editor
Melissa Burke, marketing manager
Cassandra Smith, poetry editor & book designer
Peter Burghardt, poetry editor & book designer
Sharon Zetter, poetry editor, book designer & development officer
Liza Flum, poetry editor & marketing assistant
Juliana Paslay, fiction editor
Gail Aronson, fiction editor
RJ Ingram, *OmniVerse* contributing editor
Kevin Peters, marketing assistant & *OmniVerse* Lit Scene editor
Trisha Peck, marketing assistant
Sara Burant, administrative assistant
Josie Gallup, publicity assistant
SD Sumner, publicity assistant